female

male

Red-eyed
vireo ▼●

American redstart ▼●

Hooded
warbler
▼●

Magn
warb

American
robin ▼●

Yellow-shafted
flicker
●■

White-
breasted
nuthatch
●■

Red-bellied
woodpecker ●■

Baltimore
oriole ▼●

CANADA

NORTH AMERICA

UNITED STATES
OF AMERICA

MEXICO

Pacific Ocean

FLUTE'S JOURNEY SOUTH

Gulf of
Mexico

Yucatán
Peninsula

Caribbean
Sea

CENTRAL AMERICA

Blue jay
●■

Rufous-sided
towhee ●■

Pileated
woodpecker
●■

Wood thrush
▼●

Black-and-white warbler ▼

Kentucky warbler ▼

White-eyed vireo ▼●

Northern cardinal ●■

Nebraska

Iowa

Pennsylvania

Illinois   Indiana   Ohio

Maryland/
Belt Woods

Kansas   Missouri

West
Virginia

Virginia

Kentucky

Oklahoma   Tennessee

North
Carolina

Arkansas

South
Carolina

Mississippi

Texas   Alabama   Georgia

Atlantic
Ocean

Louisiana

Florida

Gulf of Mexico

MEXICO

Atlantic Ocean

Downy woodpecker ●■

Scarlet tanager ▼●

Ovenbird ▼●

BIRDS OF THE BELT WOODS

▼ Migrates through the woods

● Nests in the woods

■ Year-round resident of the woods

▼■ Cedar waxwing

▼ Cerulean warbler

Brown-headed cowbird ■

male

On a still, starry fall evening, if you listen carefully, you may hear the calls of hundreds of migratory songbirds as they fly overhead on their journey south to the tropical rain forests. Again, in the spring, you may hear them way above, returning to their nesting sites in the cool woodlands of the North.

Sheltered by the towering canopy, the bottom of these northern forests is called the understory. There, in small, young hardwood trees like beech, holly, dogwood, and tulip poplar, wood thrushes sing their rich, powerful, pure melody. Amid rushing streams, moss-covered rocks, and hundred-year-old trees that have fallen and are turning back into earth, the nesting wood thrushes face many dangers.

This is the story of the life of one wood thrush whose existence depends upon the tropical rain forest in Monteverde, Costa Rica, the northern forest of the Belt Woods in Maryland, and all the places in between.

Flute's Journey

THE LIFE OF A WOOD THRUSH

Written and illustrated by

LYNNE CHERRY

Harcourt

Orlando   Boston   Dallas   Chicago   San Diego

Visit *The Learning Site!*

www.harcourtschool.com

I would like to thank the following friends and colleagues for reading the manuscript to ensure its accuracy: Daniel Boone, conservation chair, Prince George's Audubon Society, Maryland; Sam Droege and Chandler Robbins, National Biological Service, Patuxent Wildlife Research Center, Laurel, Maryland; Doug Wechsler, Visual Resources in Ornithology, Philadelphia, Pennsylvania; Donald Messersmith, Department of Entomology, University of Maryland, College Park, Maryland; Susan Gilchrist, Wisconsin Department of Natural Resources, Research Center, Monona, Wisconsin; Helga Burre, urban master naturalist, Massachusetts Audubon Society, Lincoln, Massachusetts; Scott Robinson, Illinois Natural History Survey, Champaign, Illinois; John Rappole, Smithsonian Conservation and Research Center, Front Royal, Virginia; and Peter Stangel, National Fish and Wildlife Foundation, Washington, D.C.

I'd like to thank the following people and organizations for helping with my research: Gene Morton, Lisa Petit, John Sterling, Mary Deinlein, Smithsonian Migratory Bird Center, National Zoo, Washington, D.C.; Ken Rosenberg, Project Tanager, Cornell Lab of Ornithology, Ithaca, New York; Dr. Roland Roth, Department of Entomology and Applied Ecology, University of Delaware, Newark, Delaware; and many members of the Maryland Ornithological Society, Annapolis, Maryland.

Special thanks to Mi Kim, for taking me out into the forest to study wood thrushes; to Chris Swarth of the Jug Bay Wetlands Sanctuary, Lothian, Maryland, for introducing me to mist-netting and bird-banding; to Ben and Lauren, who posed for me; and especially to Barbara Dowell, for sharing her vast knowledge and passion for birds.

Thank you to my friends Geoffrey Parker, Nalini Nadkarni and Jack Longino, Sue and John Trocell. Thanks to Bob Law, whose booklet *The Birds of Monteverde* proved indispensable, and to him and Susie for housing me in Monteverde. Also, thank you to the Monteverde Reserve, Ree Sheck of the Children's International Rain Forest, and La Selva Biological Research Station for facilitating my research in Costa Rica.

Thank you to the Maryland Department of Natural Resources for preserving Flute's home by saving the oldest part of the Belt Woods, and to Debbie Osborne of the Trust for Public Land, Cathy Cooper of the Episcopal Seton Belt Committee, Pam Cooper of the Western Shore Conservancy, author Tom Horton, and musician Paul Winter for their work to save the remaining 515 acres of the Belt Woods.

Also thank you to Sally Laughlin, North American Migratory Birds Curricula Assessment Project, Cambridge, Vermont; and to John Terborgh, Duke University School of Environment, Center for Tropical Biology, whose book *Where Have All the Birds Gone?* helped generate the idea for *Flute's Journey*.

And special thanks to my editor and friend, Liz Van Doren; to Helen and Herb Cherry; to Eric Fersht; and to Jasper and Rocky.

To Seton Belt,
who had the foresight to try
to protect and preserve his magnificent forest
for all time

"The one process ongoing...
that will take millions of years to correct
is the loss of genetic and species diversity
by the destruction of natural habitats.
This is a folly for which our descendants
are least likely to forgive us."

—DR. EDWARD O. WILSON

FOUR LOVELY TURQUOISE EGGS lay in a nest in a small dogwood tree in a forest in Maryland. In this nest made of leaves, mud, and fine rootlets, the eggs were warmed all day and night under the breast of the mother bird. Inside the eggs, baby wood thrushes grew until one day in May, feeling tight and squeezed, they began to peck. Each pecked and pecked until it pecked apart its eggshell and emerged into the wide world. The baby birds were tiny, wet, and featherless, naked but for a bit of down. Their eyes were closed.

The hungry
wood thrush chicks
let out shrill cries
and reached with
outstretched necks.
The parents flew
back and forth all day
bringing meals of insects and soft,
squishy worms. Eating heartily, the young birds thrived and grew.

In three days the chicks' eyes opened. Gray pinfeathers covered their
pink-and-gray skin. They began beating their small wings, strengthening
them. Seven days later, feeling squeezed in the nest that was now too small
for them, the chicks hopped to its edge and out onto the branches of the
dogwood tree, beginning to explore their world.

The chicks tried out their wings, fluttering from one branch to
another, then to the ground and back again. They had left the nest; they had
fledged. But still, whenever they were hungry, the chicks would call, and
their parents would find and feed them.

Deep in this ancient forest known as the Belt Woods, the young wood
thrushes were safe from most dangers. Cats and raccoons would not bother
them here. But they kept alert for hawks, black snakes, foxes, and people—
particularly two children who came every day to watch them quietly.

Three of the young wood thrushes and their parents kept their distance

from the children. But one of the fledglings, who had a few unusual white feathers on his head, flew closer and closer to them each day. The children named this bold young wood thrush Flute, for they knew that when he grew up he would sing as beautifully as his father and that his song would echo through the forest like the clear, sweet music of a flute.

For three weeks after he had fledged, Flute's parents continued to feed him. During July and August, his baby feathers fell out and in their place grew the long and lustrous feathers of a handsome juvenile. Now whenever Flute or his siblings came around, they were chased off by their parents, who knew that their youngsters had learned to take care of themselves.

September came and a cool breeze ruffled Flute's feathers. Autumn leaves turned gold, red, and yellow. The shorter days and the dwindling light

gave the birds the urge for going. Flute ate as many berries and insects as he could find and stored up fat—energy for the long flight ahead.

Then, one evening, as if a message was carried on the wind, Flute and many other wood thrushes lifted up from the forest and took to the air. The stream of songbirds flew south, joined along the way by other streams, until a river of migrating birds traveled together through the night, thousands of feet above the ground, protected from hawks by the darkness.

As morning light made the birds visible to predators, Flute looked down at the land. He saw thick woods below him and flew down to find cover and to feed upon insects, snails, and slugs on the forest floor. He gorged on spicebush and dogwood berries and rested for three days, then continued at night on his long journey.

The following dawn, Flute flew low, looking for a woods with berry bushes. But where there had once been forest, for miles he saw only paved roads and suburban development. Finally he saw below him a spicebush grove planted around a school by children who wanted to help migratory songbirds. He flew down and fed to his heart's content.

Flute took to the air again, and in several days he reached High Island, off the coast of Texas. There he joined throngs of other birds. The thicket rang with birdcalls as the birds feasted to store up energy for their flight across the Gulf of Mexico. One night, in a huge burst, Flute left land and flew in the same direction as the winds. He flew for twenty straight hours, for six hundred miles over the water, until he arrived on the Yucatán Peninsula in Mexico, where he rested and fed.

Many of the migrating birds stopped in Mexico to spend the winter. But for another week, Flute continued south through the forests of Central America, feeding along the way. Finally he arrived in the Monteverde rain forest in Costa Rica, where his ancestors had come every winter for generations.

Migratory songbirds from all over North America congregated on this green mountain while others just passed through the Monteverde forest on their way to their wintering grounds farther south. Some of the birds were Flute's neighbors from home in the Belt Woods. Other migrants had come from different parts of North America and were unfamiliar to Flute.

In Monteverde, while Flute was trying to find a suitable place to live, he joined flocks of tropical birds that live in Costa Rica year-round. These indigenous birds never fly north. But here in the tropical rain forest there was food enough for all.

After searching for several days, Flute found an unoccupied tree at the edge of the forest. He made sounds like *chur chur chur* and a bold *rat-tat-tat* to warn other wood thrushes to keep away from the territory he had claimed as his own.

From October through March, as snow fell in the cold north, Flute was warm and well fed in the Monteverde forest. In the cool mornings, Flute tossed dry leaves to find the tasty insects underneath. In the heat of the day, he took a siesta—a rest. Each afternoon, at precisely four o'clock, he visited a birdbath in a yard at the edge of the forest preserve.

This forest is called the Bosque Eterno de los Niños (the Eternal Forest of the Children). Many forests in Costa Rica are being cut down, but children from all over the world have raised funds to help preserve this one as a home for the songbirds and the other forest creatures.

Soon after Flute's arrival, another wood thrush came to the Monteverde forest. He had arrived late in Costa Rica and found his former winter home

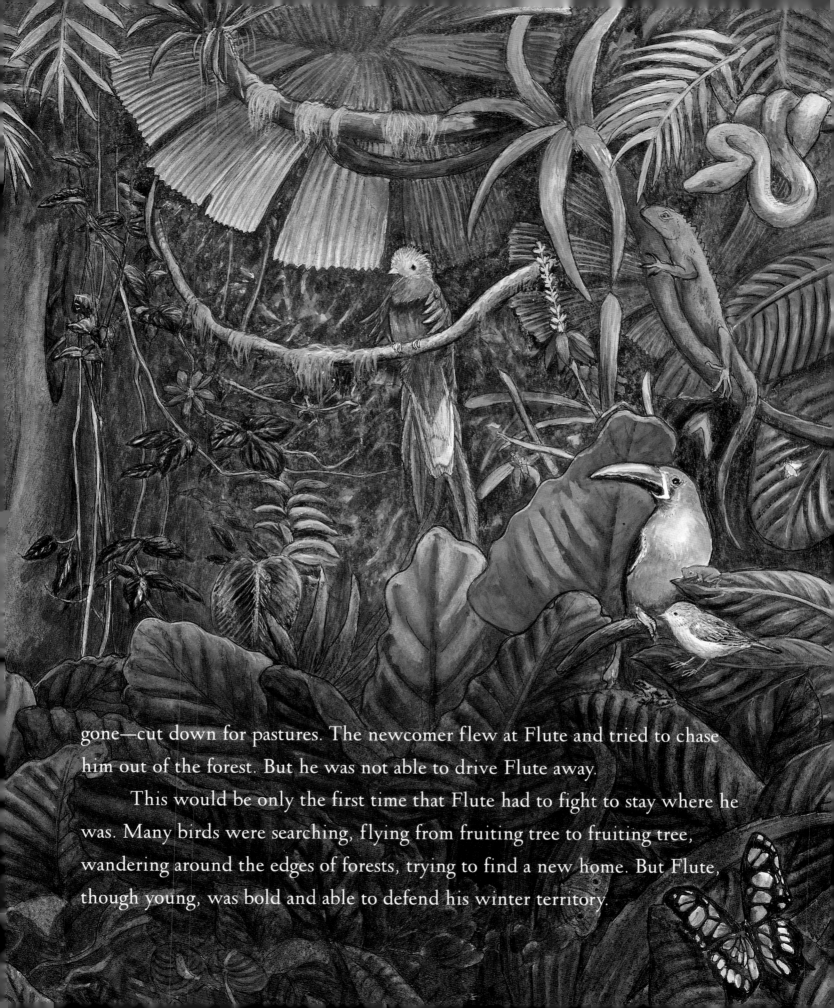

gone—cut down for pastures. The newcomer flew at Flute and tried to chase
him out of the forest. But he was not able to drive Flute away.

    This would be only the first time that Flute had to fight to stay where he
was. Many birds were searching, flying from fruiting tree to fruiting tree,
wandering around the edges of forests, trying to find a new home. But Flute,
though young, was bold and able to defend his winter territory.

In the North, longer days heralded spring's arrival. Flute, now full grown, felt an urge to return to his Maryland forest. So one day in March, with hundreds of other birds, he took to the sky. He flew along the Yucatán and, again, made the arduous crossing of the Gulf of Mexico. After resting in Texas, Flute headed northeast through Louisiana, Mississippi, Alabama, Georgia, and the Carolinas.

Plants and flowers, responding to the increased light, were opening their buds after a winter's dormancy. Caterpillar eggs hatched and their larvae began to eat the tender young leaves. Insects, hiding under dead leaves, came out of their winter sleep. The migrating birds followed the leafing-out of the trees and plants and ate caterpillars, grubs, and other insects along their way.

For generations the migrating wood thrushes had stopped to feed in a forest of mature beech, poplar, and oak trees in South Carolina. But now much of this forest was being logged. Instead of being hidden deep in woodlands, Flute had to forage at the edge of clear-cuts. As he fed, Flute noticed a dark shadow growing larger and larger around him. A hawk swooped toward him. Flute flew up only seconds before the hawk's sharp talons hit the ground.

At Flute's stopover in North Carolina, he found a new road and houses being built in what had been acres of untouched forest only a few months before. Flute foraged for beetles, snails, slugs, and spiders in the leaf litter on the edge of a green lawn. But chemicals sprayed on the lawn had washed into the leaves and onto the insects that hid under them.

That night, when it came time to rise up into the sky, Flute felt ill and lethargic. He could not lift his wings to fly. Instead he sat shivering on the forest floor throughout the night and all the next day. It was not until the following night that Flute felt well enough to eat again. As he ate, gaining back his strength, he noticed a sudden movement in the underbrush. Then a cat pounced! Flute burst into the air just in time, and the cat caught only tail feathers.

Flute arrived in the Belt Woods in late April. But upon approaching this old-growth forest where he was hatched, he became confused. Many of the landmarks he knew were gone. Most of the forest along one side of the Belt Woods had been cut down, and many homes were being built. A road snaked through a new development.

Flute flew down and found the dogwood tree where he had once been a turquoise egg in a nest. He was about to alight on a branch when another, older wood thrush swooped down and chased him off. Flute tried to claim several other nesting sites, but other birds, already defending them, chased him away.

Flute finally found his own spot in a small tulip poplar. He sat quite erect and effortlessly emitted the wonderful notes of his song. "E-olee!" he sang, and rested; then he sang a trill. The powerful, pure melody followed, vibrating intermittently like a bell throughout the forest. The song rose and fell, swelled and died away, until night had fallen. It was the most beautiful sound in the forest.

At daybreak Flute again began singing. The two children had been waiting for the return of their friend, and when they heard the beautiful song echoing through the woods, they followed it to the foot of the tulip poplar. There Flute was singing to attract a female wood thrush with whom to mate and build a nest. And soon she appeared. The children named her Feather, for she sat before Flute, fluffed her feathers, raised her wings, and then took off in a rapid circular flight. In swift pursuit Flute followed Feather's twisting and turning through the forest shadows.

Flute and Feather fed together, and then with weeds, grass, leaves, mud, and fine rootlets, they built a nest in the tulip poplar sapling. Several days later it held three blue eggs.

That night, while Flute and Feather were sleeping, a big black snake slithered up the tree and ate one of their eggs. The next night a raccoon climbed the tree, and although they tried, Flute and Feather could not chase the intruder away. Holding the last two eggs in its small paws, the raccoon cracked and ate them while the nest fell, in pieces, to the forest floor.

Several days later
Flute followed Feather
again, flying wildly
through the forest. In
a small beech tree close
to the forest's edge, they
built a new nest. A week
later Feather laid four turquoise eggs.
As Flute flew in and out of the beech tree, a female
brown-headed cowbird watched. She waited for a moment
when both wood thrushes were away. Then she flew to their nest, punctured
one of the eggs, and carried it away. Early the next morning, when Flute and
Feather were again away from the nest, the cowbird deposited her own white
egg with brown speckles in its place.

Eleven days later a gray chick emerged from the brown-speckled egg. The next day three wood thrushes hatched from the turquoise eggs. During the following days the four chicks cheeped to attract the attention of Flute and Feather. But the cowbird chick chirped loudest and stuck its neck out longest. More of the food brought by Flute and Feather went into its mouth, while the wood thrush chicks got less and less. Two of the wood thrushes grew, fledged, and flew as their father had the year before, but one was too weak to survive because most of the food meant for it had been fed to the loud cowbird chick.

When Flute's nestlings were grown and old enough to care for themselves, he and Feather chased them away. The young cowbird flew off to join the flock of cowbirds that lived in the open area next to the forest. There they thrived on the insects that lived in the suburban lawns. The two wood thrush chicks stayed in the woods and practiced flipping over the dead leaves on the forest floor to find the insects underneath.

Every day the children watched Flute, Feather, and their brood flourishing in the Belt Woods. They listened, enchanted, as Flute's haunting flutelike music rose and fell, swelled and died away, harmonizing with the songs of the ovenbirds and the vireos, the chattering of chipmunks, and the breeze whispering through the leaves of this summer forest.

When the days grew shorter and cooler again, the children watched Flute and his family leave on their journey south. They hoped that the wood thrushes would avoid all perils and make it safely back to the Belt Woods the next spring—and for many springs to come.

Author's Note

LIKE FLUTE and other wood thrushes, birds that migrate face many dangers. Hawks, cats, and owls prey on adult birds; snakes, chipmunks, squirrels, raccoons, crows, and blue jays eat their eggs. Cowbirds destroy wood thrush eggs, removing them from wood thrush nests and replacing them with their own eggs. But habitat loss, in both North and South America, is one of the most serious problems migratory birds face. However, many people have been successful in saving habitats such as native forests. Children from around the world have preserved more than forty thousand acres in the Monteverde rain forest, and children have also helped to save land in other parts of the world, including their own communities.

Flute's spring nesting ground and summer home is in the Belt Woods in Maryland. This old-growth forest was loved by Seton Belt, whose family had owned it since colonial times. Before his death he willed his land in trust to the Episcopal Church in Washington, D.C., and St. Barnabas Church in Maryland, with the understanding that the property would not be sold nor the forests cut. Unfortunately, the Episcopal Church went to court to have the will modified and received approval to sell the land. As this book went to press, environmental organizations and various individuals, including some members of the Episcopal Church, had won the fight to have the land preserved. Now both Flute's northern and southern homes are preserved.

Here are some of the things that you can do to help migratory birds survive:

- Keep cats indoors during nesting season.
- Discourage your family and neighbors from using pesticides.
- Create new habitat by planting native berry bushes and trees where migratory birds may feed and nest.
- Preserve existing habitat by working to protect and preserve tracts of mature woods.

Talk with adults in your community who are interested in land preservation and have them help you identify land that might be preserved. You can also write letters to politicians, your local zoning board, and your local land preservation trust to find out what you can do to help.

For more information about how to make the world safer for songbirds and save land in your own community, write to: Save the Land You Love, The Center for Children's Environmental Literature, P.O. Box 5995, Washington, D.C. 20016.

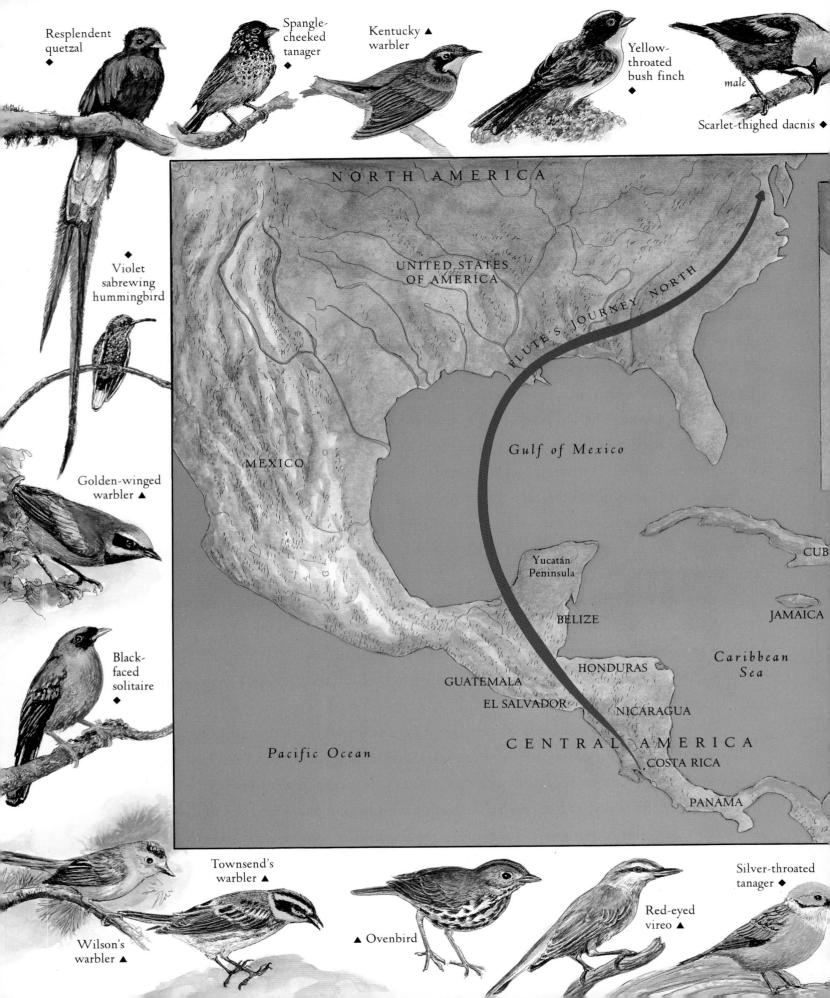

Resplendent quetzal ◆

Spangle-cheeked tanager ◆

Kentucky warbler ▲

Yellow-throated bush finch ◆

Scarlet-thighed dacnis ◆
male

Violet sabrewing hummingbird ◆

Golden-winged warbler ▲

Black-faced solitaire ◆

NORTH AMERICA

UNITED STATES OF AMERICA

FLUTE'S JOURNEY NORTH

MEXICO

Gulf of Mexico

Yucatán Peninsula

BELIZE

GUATEMALA

EL SALVADOR

HONDURAS

NICARAGUA

CENTRAL AMERICA

COSTA RICA

PANAMA

Pacific Ocean

Caribbean Sea

CUB[A]

JAMAICA

Wilson's warbler ▲

Townsend's warbler ▲

▲ Ovenbird

Red-eyed vireo ▲

Silver-throated tanager ◆

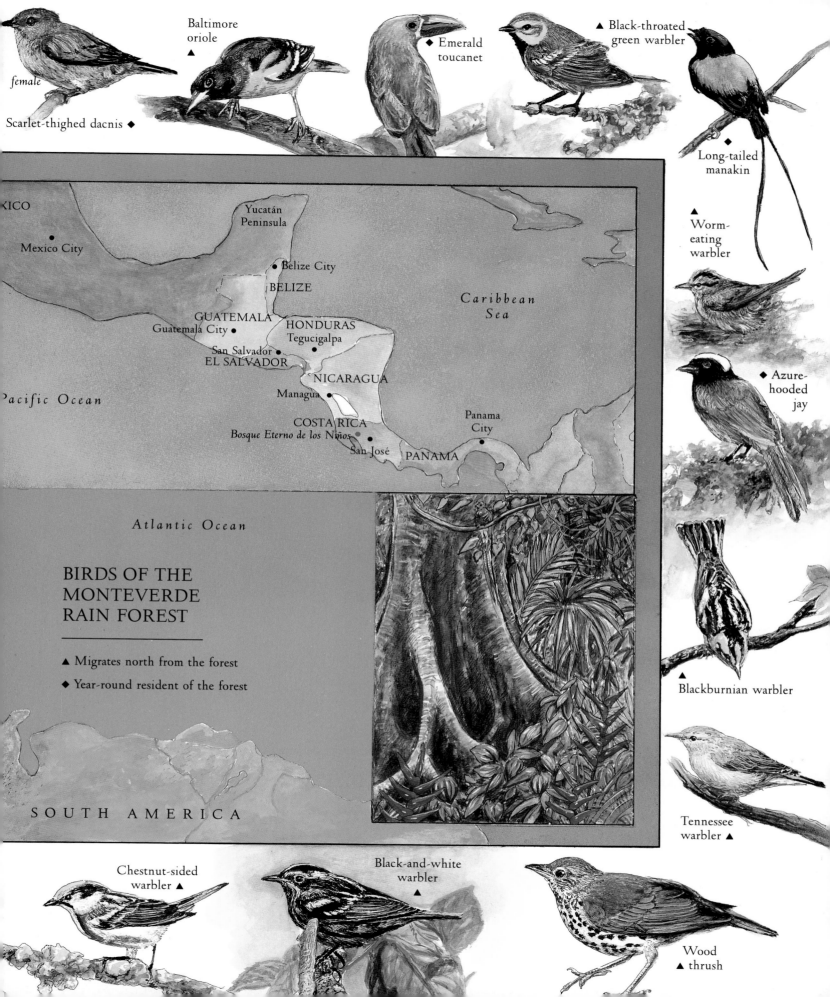

female

Scarlet-thighed dacnis ◆

Baltimore oriole ▲

◆ Emerald toucanet

▲ Black-throated green warbler

◆ Long-tailed manakin

▲ Worm-eating warbler

◆ Azure-hooded jay

▲ Blackburnian warbler

Tennessee warbler ▲

BIRDS OF THE MONTEVERDE RAIN FOREST

▲ Migrates north from the forest

◆ Year-round resident of the forest

Atlantic Ocean

SOUTH AMERICA

XICO
Mexico City

Yucatán Peninsula

Belize City

BELIZE

GUATEMALA
Guatemala City

HONDURAS
Tegucigalpa

San Salvador
EL SALVADOR

NICARAGUA
Managua

Caribbean Sea

Pacific Ocean

COSTA RICA
Bosque Eterno de los Niños
San José

Panama City

PANAMA

Chestnut-sided warbler ▲

Black-and-white warbler ▲

Wood thrush ▲

Flute's Journey: The Life of a Wood Thrush by Lynne Cherry.
Copyright © 1997 by Lynne Cherry. Reprinted by permission of Harcourt, Inc.

Printed in Singapore

ISBN 0-15-314369-X

3 4 5 6 7 8 9 10 068 03 02 01